this journal belongs to...

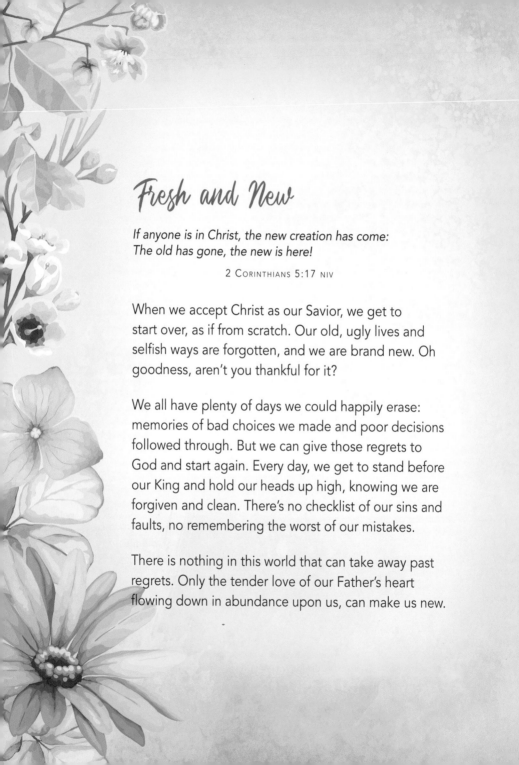

Fresh and New

If anyone is in Christ, the new creation has come:
The old has gone, the new is here!

2 CORINTHIANS 5:17 NIV

When we accept Christ as our Savior, we get to start over, as if from scratch. Our old, ugly lives and selfish ways are forgotten, and we are brand new. Oh goodness, aren't you thankful for it?

We all have plenty of days we could happily erase: memories of bad choices we made and poor decisions followed through. But we can give those regrets to God and start again. Every day, we get to stand before our King and hold our heads up high, knowing we are forgiven and clean. There's no checklist of our sins and faults, no remembering the worst of our mistakes.

There is nothing in this world that can take away past regrets. Only the tender love of our Father's heart flowing down in abundance upon us, can make us new.

How do you feel when you think of God's love
washing over you and making you new?

_____

_____

_____

_____

_____

_____

_____

_____

_____

_____

_____

_____

_____

_____

_____

_____

_____

_____

_____

_____

_____

_____

The Father's Love

"If a man has a hundred sheep but one of the sheep gets lost, he will leave the other ninety-nine on the hill and go to look for the lost sheep. I tell you the truth, if he finds it he is happier about that one sheep than about the ninety-nine that were never lost."

MATTHEW 18:12-13 NCV

Regardless of how beautifully or how imperfectly your earthly father showed his love, your heavenly Father's love is utterly boundless. Rest in that thought a moment. There is nothing you can do to change how he feels about you. Nothing.

We spend so much time trying to make ourselves more lovable, from beauty regimens to gourmet baking, to being there for pretty much everyone. It's easy to forget we are already perfectly loved. Our Father loves us more than we can imagine, and he would do anything for us.

You might have had a rough day or a really good day. Remember that your heavenly Father has been loving you throughout your day. Who do you love most fiercely, most protectively, most desperately here on earth? What would you do for them? Know that it's a mere fraction, nearly immeasurable, of what God would do for you. Spend some time thanking him for his great love.

Are there areas of your life that you feel lost in?

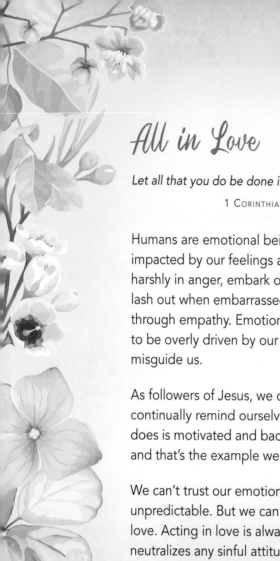

All in Love

Let all that you do be done in love.

1 CORINTHIANS 16:14 ESV

Humans are emotional beings. We are motivated and impacted by our feelings and those of others. We speak harshly in anger, embark on adventures because of curiosity, lash out when embarrassed, and give to those in need through empathy. Emotion is a gift, but if we allow ourselves to be overly driven by our human passions, they will misguide us.

As followers of Jesus, we can check our hearts and continually remind ourselves to act in love. Everything God does is motivated and backed by overwhelming love for us, and that's the example we should follow.

We can't trust our emotions to drive us—they are too unpredictable. But we can choose to do everything in love. Acting in love is always the right course of action; it neutralizes any sinful attitude or motivation. The positive effect of love on our lives is undeniable; love brings us closer to God and more into his likeness. As we become more like him, we are able to choose love over other emotions that spring up so quickly.

How do you take control over your emotions and choose to love?

_____
_____
_____
_____
_____
_____
_____
_____
_____
_____
_____
_____
_____
_____
_____
_____
_____
_____
_____
_____
_____
_____
_____
_____

Powerful Kindness

I will tell about the L<small>ORD</small>'s kindness
and praise him for everything he has done.
I will praise the L<small>ORD</small> for the many good things he has given us
and for his goodness to the people of Israel.
He has shown great mercy to us
and has been very kind to us.

<small>ISAIAH 63:7 NCV</small>

The Bible says that the kindness of the Lord leads people to repentance: not his anger, not his wrath—his kindness. There is power in kindness: a power that moves souls and changes lives. We can subconsciously equate kindness with weakness, but it's the exact opposite.

We can trust God and turn to him often, confident that his mercy is present, even in suffering. The Israelites turned their backs on God too many times to count. But what we see time and time again in their story is that God was still good. He showed them mercy; he gave them good things. He was kind to them.

Of course, Israel wasn't spared consequences and trials, but the people knew God's promises and trusted him. In the same way, we can trust God and turn to him often, confident that his mercy is present, even in suffering.

How can you see God's goodness in your life
even through the consequences of your choices?

_____
_____
_____
_____
_____
_____
_____
_____
_____
_____
_____
_____
_____
_____
_____
_____
_____
_____
_____
_____
_____
_____
_____

The Fear Factor

When I am afraid, I will put my trust in you.
I praise God for what he has promised.
I trust in God, so why should I be afraid?

PSALM 56:3-4 NLT

David did not hesitate to admit when he was afraid!
King Saul was pursuing him and so great was his terror
that he ran to the enemy's camp—an unlikely place
to find refuge. It was bold and risky, but perhaps King
Achish would not recognize him, or might consider him a
deserter and an asset.

Unfortunately, David was found out, reported to the king,
and, motivated by more fear, acted like a mad man and was
sent away. Fear causes us to do things we normally would
not. It wasn't long before David readjusted his thinking and
put his trust once again in God. It is interesting that he says,
"When I am afraid," not "If I am afraid." David knew he
would experience fear again.

Fear is a human response, and unless counteracted
by trust, is destructive at best. What are you afraid
of this evening? Are you magnifying a concern into
an impossible mountain of what ifs? Trust Jesus.
Remember his promises to you. No matter the
outcome, he is in charge!

What are you afraid of today?
Can you choose to trust God instead?

_____

_____

_____

_____

_____

_____

_____

_____

_____

_____

_____

_____

_____

_____

_____

_____

_____

_____

_____

_____

_____

_____

_____

No Words

They sat on the ground with him for seven days and nights. No one said a word to Job, for they saw that his suffering was too great for words.

JOB 2:13 NLT

We recognize Job as a person who suffered greatly. It might be easier to identify with Job because we have all experienced suffering in our lives. But what about being a friend of a person who is suffering?

We love to talk, don't we? Words of encouragement, words of comfort, words of advice. Even if you are the quiet type, you know someone who is rarely at a loss for words. It can be all too easy to try and talk, but sometimes we just need to be near to those who need it. Sometimes our support is shown in actions not words. Occasionally, there really are no words. Someone you love is hurting, and you truly don't know what to say. Your presence says it all. Know that, in those moments you feel lost for words, if God occupies the central place in your heart, he'll make your heart known.

How easy or difficult would it be for you to simply be with someone in their sorrow and not try to "fix" them? Spend some time reflecting on the friends who have done exactly that for you and be thankful for the support of good people.

Who would be blessed by your silent, loving presence?
Do you need that from someone today?

_____

_____

_____

_____

_____

_____

_____

_____

_____

_____

_____

_____

_____

_____

_____

_____

_____

_____

_____

_____

_____

_____

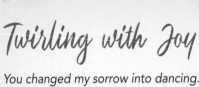

Twirling with Joy

You changed my sorrow into dancing.
You took away my clothes of sadness,
and clothed me in happiness.
I will sing to you and not be silent.
LORD, my God, I will praise you forever.

PSALM 30:11-12 NCV

Abandoned, abused single mother finds love, purpose, and healing. That's a movie most of us would watch. Who doesn't love a good restoration story? When God heals broken places and redeems lost situations, our hearts swell with possibility. If he can restore her life, he can surely come in and fix mine.

It's true. The mourners will dance, clothed in happiness. Voices silenced by sadness will sing loudest songs of praise. And you, regardless of what you face now, will be there: twirling with joy, singing your heart out. You will be there.

When we give God a chance to change our outlook for the day, he will gladly step in and do it. We don't need to focus on our sadness. In fact, we should be shouting his praises from the ends of the earth. Even when we feel surrounded by grief, we can trust God to change us into our party clothes! There is an abundance of joy in his presence. We just need to spend time there to find it.

What can you praise God for today?

_____
_____
_____
_____
_____
_____
_____
_____
_____
_____
_____
_____
_____
_____
_____
_____
_____
_____
_____
_____
_____
_____
_____
_____

Follow the Arrow

Your ears shall hear a word behind you, saying,
"This is the way, walk in it,"
Whenever you turn to the right hand
Or whenever you turn to the left.

ISAIAH 30:21 NKJV

Decisions, decisions. It seems a week never goes by without our needing to make at least one important choice. Whether job related, relationship motivated, or something as seemingly innocent as how to spend a free Friday, wouldn't it be nice to have an arrow pointing us in the right direction—especially if we are in danger of making a wrong turn?

According to the Word, we have exactly that. When we truly desire to walk the path God sets us on, and when we earnestly seek his voice, he promises to lead us in the right direction.

Consider the decisions you have had to make today. What decisions will you need to make tomorrow? Whether you choose the right or the left, know that God is able to guide you into his best for the situation. You might not get it right every time, but his ever-present Spirit is there, ready to put you back on the path each time you wander off.

What guidance do you need right now?

_____

_____

_____

_____

_____

_____

_____

_____

_____

_____

_____

_____

_____

_____

_____

_____

_____

_____

_____

_____

_____

Beyond Your Sight

From the ends of the earth,
I cry to you for help
when my heart is overwhelmed.
Lead me to the towering rock of safety.

PSALM 61:2 NLT

Have you ever wandered through a maze? Even though you may be good at solving mazes on paper, moving through shrubbery or stalks of corn at ground level you are bound to run into a dead end or two. If only there were a place to climb up high and see the way through.

So what can you do? Call for help. Follow the voice of someone who can see more than you. Today as you run into situations that require a better view, ask God to guide you. He loves to answer those prayers! When life feels like a maze, and you're faint from the exhaustion of running into walls, call out to God. Follow the sound of his voice to the next turn. Allow his hand to lift you up—beyond your own sight—and show you the way through.

Do you know that God is your towering rock of safety? He is always listening, waiting to guide you through the overwhelming situations in your life. Call out to him whenever you need help. He will not let you down.

Do you find it easy to ask God for help?
Why do you think this is?

_____

_____

_____

_____

_____

_____

_____

_____

_____

_____

_____

_____

_____

_____

_____

_____

_____

_____

_____

_____

_____

_____

_____

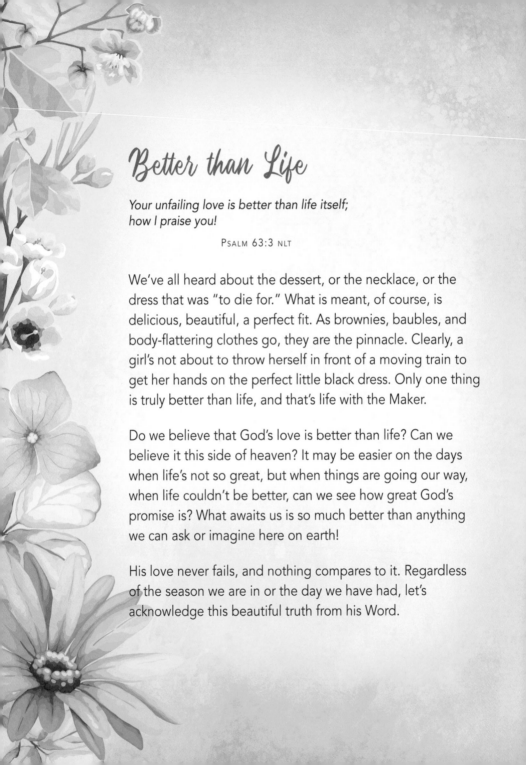

Better than Life

Your unfailing love is better than life itself;
how I praise you!

PSALM 63:3 NLT

We've all heard about the dessert, or the necklace, or the dress that was "to die for." What is meant, of course, is delicious, beautiful, a perfect fit. As brownies, baubles, and body-flattering clothes go, they are the pinnacle. Clearly, a girl's not about to throw herself in front of a moving train to get her hands on the perfect little black dress. Only one thing is truly better than life, and that's life with the Maker.

Do we believe that God's love is better than life? Can we believe it this side of heaven? It may be easier on the days when life's not so great, but when things are going our way, when life couldn't be better, can we see how great God's promise is? What awaits us is so much better than anything we can ask or imagine here on earth!

His love never fails, and nothing compares to it. Regardless of the season we are in or the day we have had, let's acknowledge this beautiful truth from his Word.

Can you believe in your heart that
God's love is better than life itself?

_____
_____
_____
_____
_____
_____
_____
_____
_____
_____
_____
_____
_____
_____
_____
_____
_____
_____
_____
_____

Inherent Goodness

*You, O L*ORD*, are good and forgiving,*
abounding in steadfast love to all who call upon you.

PSALM 86:5 ESV

We all approach God for different reasons, with different matters on our hearts. Sometimes, we come to him in joy and thankfulness. Other times, we come with our heads bowed low, nearly crushed by shame and sorrow. No matter how we come to God, he meets us the same way—with goodness.

God is full of love for us, his children. He doesn't receive us with quick anger or frustration, but with a love that is steadfast and unchanging. God isn't just good some of the time; goodness is his nature. Whether he is passing righteous judgment or granting undeserved grace, he is good. Because of his perfect character, we can wholly trust him.

As you move through your days, make a point of seeing God's goodness in your life.

How did you see God's goodness manifested in your life today?

_____

_____

_____

_____

_____

_____

_____

_____

_____

_____

_____

_____

_____

_____

_____

_____

_____

_____

_____

_____

_____

_____

Cherished

I am convinced that neither death nor life, neither angels nor demons, neither the present nor the future, nor any powers, neither height nor depth, nor anything else in all creation, will be able to separate us from the love of God that is in Christ Jesus our Lord.

ROMANS 8:38-39 NIV

It's good to be loved, isn't it? What feeling really compares to knowing someone has run through the rain, cancelled an international flight, driven all night—for you? Even if we've never experienced it, we've imagined it in our hearts. Or else we've had the realization that we, too, would move heaven and earth for the one we love the most. Whether spouse, child, parent, sibling, or dear friend, to love and be loved deeply may be the best feeling there is.

Remember that Jesus loves you even more than this. No matter what you face as you get going this morning, be assured that you are loved by the most perfect love there is. How much love you have given or received is a mere sampling of the way Jesus feels about you. You are cherished, loved beyond reason or measure. The one who really can move heaven and earth would do so in a heartbeat—for you.

Have you seen God's love for you today? Have you been able to recognize his voice despite all the chaos and noise in your life? Let the incredible words of this Scripture wash over you as you realize there is nothing—absolutely nothing—Jesus wouldn't do for you.

When do you feel most separated from God?
How can you assure yourself of his love in these times?

_____

_____

_____

_____

_____

_____

_____

_____

_____

_____

_____

_____

_____

_____

_____

_____

_____

_____

_____

_____

_____

Heavenly Rewards

Be patient, therefore, brothers, until the coming of the Lord.
See how the farmer waits for the precious fruit of the earth,
being patient about it, until it receives the early and the late rains.

JAMES 5:7 ESV

There is a prevalent message in today's culture that whispers sweet and appealing lies: rights to luxury and self-indulgence. You deserve it, Christian! God wants you to have it and to be happy. This whisper takes away the sweet truth of a God who rewards us and injects the poisonous lie that that enjoyment must be immediate.

God wants to reward you. That is truth. He promises rewards to the faithful, and he keeps his promises. Those rewards are often not on this earth, and why would we want them to be? Earthly rewards are enjoyable, but they can be destroyed by moth and rust. Heaven's treasures are eternal.

To lean into the pull of God's kingdom instead of the tug of instant gratification, requires enduring patience. When you are tempted to give in to temporary satisfaction, remember the rewards that wait for you in heaven. Know that your loving Father is waiting to give you more than you could think to ask for. Let that spur you on in your works and actions, motivating you to live with a kingdom-driven mind-set.

What do you find it most difficult to be satisfied with in your life right now?

_____

_____

_____

_____

_____

_____

_____

_____

_____

_____

_____

_____

_____

_____

_____

_____

_____

_____

_____

_____

_____

_____

Troubled Heart

"Peace I leave with you; my peace I give you.
I do not give to you as the world gives.
Do not let your hearts be troubled and do not be afraid."

JOHN 14:27 NIV

We all go through seasons where it seems every corner hides a new challenge to our serenity, assuming we've actually achieved any semblance of serenity in the first place. Why is it so hard to find peace in this world? Because we're looking in this world. True peace is found in Jesus. There will be a lot of things that try to take away your sense of peace, but if you allow the Holy Spirit to speak to you, your days will be filled with moments of knowing that he is near.

After his resurrection, before Jesus ascended into heaven, he left his disciples with something they'd never had before: peace. More specifically, he gave them his peace, a gift not of this world. Whatever the world can offer us can also be taken from us. Any security, happiness, or temporary reprieve from suffering is just that: temporary. Only the things of heaven are permanent and cannot be taken away.

Do not let your heart be troubled, Jesus tells us. This means we have a choice. Share the things with him that threaten your peace, and then remember they have no hold on you. You are his, and his peace is yours.

What have you been troubled about lately?
Will you allow God's peace to replace your fear?

_____
_____
_____
_____
_____
_____
_____
_____
_____
_____
_____
_____
_____
_____
_____
_____
_____
_____
_____
_____
_____
_____
_____

Hearing God

Faith comes from hearing,
and hearing through the word of Christ.

ROMANS 10:17 ESV

The best way to know if something is true, or right, is to hear it for yourself—straight from the source. You believe you nailed the interview, but you don't believe you got the job until you get the phone call. You feel you might be pregnant, but you wait for the test results before telling anyone. The same is true for bad news, at least ideally. You get wind of a rumor about a friend's indiscretion, but you wait for her side of the story before believing a word.

What about God? How can we hear from him? How do we discern his will for our lives? We may not have a hotline, but we do have his book. God speaks to us through his Word, so if you are waiting for confirmation, direction, validation, or conviction, pick it up. Read, and listen.

How often do you feel God speaking to you through his Word? Were your conversations today as frequent and meaningful as you'd like? Share your heart with him and listen for his reply.

What do you hear God saying to you?

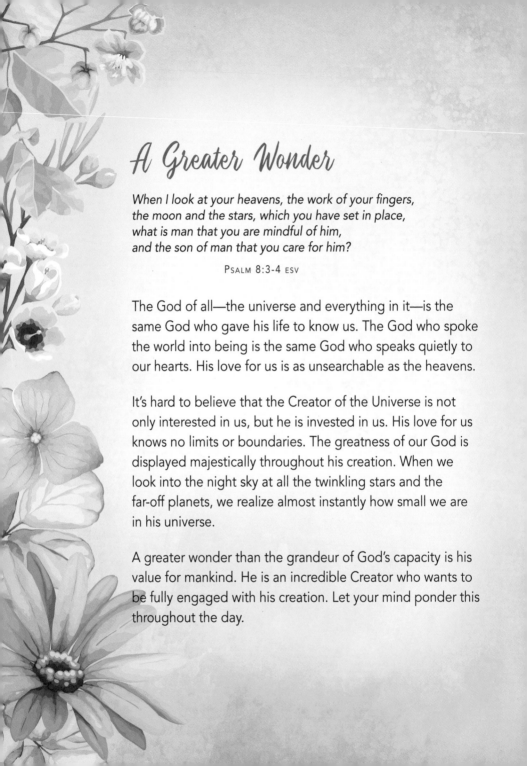

A Greater Wonder

When I look at your heavens, the work of your fingers,
the moon and the stars, which you have set in place,
what is man that you are mindful of him,
and the son of man that you care for him?

PSALM 8:3-4 ESV

The God of all—the universe and everything in it—is the same God who gave his life to know us. The God who spoke the world into being is the same God who speaks quietly to our hearts. His love for us is as unsearchable as the heavens.

It's hard to believe that the Creator of the Universe is not only interested in us, but he is invested in us. His love for us knows no limits or boundaries. The greatness of our God is displayed majestically throughout his creation. When we look into the night sky at all the twinkling stars and the far-off planets, we realize almost instantly how small we are in his universe.

A greater wonder than the grandeur of God's capacity is his value for mankind. He is an incredible Creator who wants to be fully engaged with his creation. Let your mind ponder this throughout the day.

Spend time pondering the majesty of God's creation and the wonder of his desire to be directly involved in it.

_____

_____

_____

_____

_____

_____

_____

_____

_____

_____

_____

_____

_____

_____

_____

_____

_____

_____

_____

_____

_____

_____

_____

_____

_____

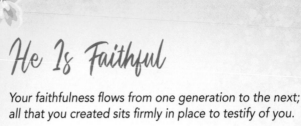

He Is Faithful

Your faithfulness flows from one generation to the next;
all that you created sits firmly in place to testify of you.

PSALM 119:90 TPT

What is the oldest thing you own? How long have you had it, and what does it mean to you? Whether a decades-old diamond ring, twenty-year-old car, or a tattered baby blanket hanging together by threads, you probably know it won't last forever.

How about your longest relationship? How many years have you been connected to this person through the good and the bad? One way we decide where to place our faith is longevity. History matters. You can carry on the faithfulness of the generations even as you go about your day. Take Jesus with you in your heart and actions.

Consider now what God made: the earth we live on. Scientists estimate it to be 4.5 billion years old, give or take fifty million. Whether we think it's been around that long or six to ten thousand years, it's some quality workmanship. If we're looking for someone to trust, we won't find better credentials than that. Through every storm, every disaster, every war, and every attack of the enemy, our earth stands. Ponder all God has made and all he has done and share your heart with him regarding his faithfulness. Have you embraced it today?

What good things in your life have come from past generations?

_____
_____
_____
_____
_____
_____
_____
_____
_____
_____
_____
_____
_____
_____
_____
_____
_____
_____
_____
_____
_____
_____
_____

More than Gold

These troubles come to prove that your faith is pure. This purity of faith is worth more than gold, which can be proved to be pure by fire but will ruin. But the purity of your faith will bring you praise and glory and honor when Jesus Christ is shown to you.

1 Peter 1:7 NCV

We can waste much of our lives trying to answer the whys of our most difficult times. Most of the answers we seek will not be revealed to us until we meet the Lord in heaven, but Scriptures such as this one from Peter provide lovely encouragement while we wait.

We know gold is precious—so precious it's a universal standard for measuring the entire world's wealth. Here, we are told that faith that withstands troubled times is worth more than all the gold on earth. Holding strong to God's promises regardless of what struggles we face affords us an invaluable reward: the praise, honor, and glory of Jesus himself.

This doesn't mean our difficulty is a test assigned by God, but the outcome—a faith that withstands the fire—is used by him to bless us beyond imagining.

What testing do you sense in your life lately?
Can you determine to be proven genuine in your faith
throughout the testing?

_____
_____
_____
_____
_____
_____
_____
_____
_____
_____
_____
_____
_____
_____
_____
_____
_____
_____
_____
_____
_____

Remain Faithful

Hold on to loyal love and don't let go,
and be faithful to all that you've been taught.
Let your life be shaped by integrity,
with truth written upon your heart.

PROVERBS 3:3 TPT

A video of a small, white dog entering a hospital through the automatic doors and wandering its halls made national news a while ago. A short investigation revealed the dog's owner had been taken to the hospital for cancer treatment. The dog bolted from the yard earlier that day and ran all the way—nearly two miles—to the hospital to see her owner. No one is sure how she knew where to go. She was led by love.

God desires that kind of faithfulness from us. He wants his daughters to seek him, to love him, with all our hearts. May nothing stop you today from returning his faithfulness with your own! Your days may be filled with many challenges, some small, some big, but with God's truth in your heart you can have integrity in your decisions and actions.

Do you see how much your Father loves you? He desires your faithfulness so much he wants you to write it on your heart. What would it take for you to seek him intently, to bolt from the safety of your surroundings in search of him? Even—or perhaps especially—if we don't know where we are going, let us be led by love to show our faithfulness to our Father.

What areas of your life do you need to submit to his truth?
Where can you show more integrity?

_____

_____

_____

_____

_____

_____

_____

_____

_____

_____

_____

_____

_____

_____

_____

_____

_____

_____

_____

_____

_____

_____

_____

Truly Special

You are a chosen people,
a royal priesthood,
a holy nation,
God's special possession.

1 PETER 2:9 NIV

We all want to believe that we are special. Most of us grow up being told that we are, and it feels good to believe it. But over time, we look around us and realize that, really, we are just like everyone else.

Sometimes doubt creeps in, making us second guess ourselves and damaging our self-confidence. We can choose to believe that God has called and chosen us for something truly special.

Long before you were even in your mother's womb, you were set aside and marked as special. You were chosen to be God's special possession, and that's a pretty amazing thing. Of all the people in the world, God has chosen you to do something only you can do. Ask him to show you what he has for you as you continue to walk in his wonderful light.

What things can you see about yourself that are special to God?

_____
_____
_____
_____
_____
_____
_____
_____
_____
_____
_____
_____
_____
_____
_____
_____
_____
_____
_____
_____

Hope

I pray that the God who gives hope will fill you with much joy and peace while you trust in him. Then your hope will overflow by the power of the Holy Spirit.

ROMANS 15:13 NCV

What differentiates hope from a wish? Think about the lottery. Does one hope to win or wish to win? How about a promotion, a pregnancy, or a proposal? Both hoping and wishing contain desire, but for wishing, that is where it ends. Hope goes deeper. The strong desire for something good to happen is coupled with a reason to believe that it will.

We see how vital hope is, and why it's such a beautiful gift. Desire without hope is empty, but together they bring joy, expectancy, and peace. When we put our hope in Christ, he becomes our reason to believe good things will happen. Has he been your hope today?

Allow the blessing from this Scripture to wash over you as the Holy Spirit reminds you of the hope, joy, and peace he brings. Believe good things will happen—you have a wonderful reason to.

Where or when have you seen God bless you with his joy and peace lately?

_____

_____

_____

_____

_____

_____

_____

_____

_____

_____

_____

_____

_____

_____

_____

_____

_____

_____

_____

_____

_____

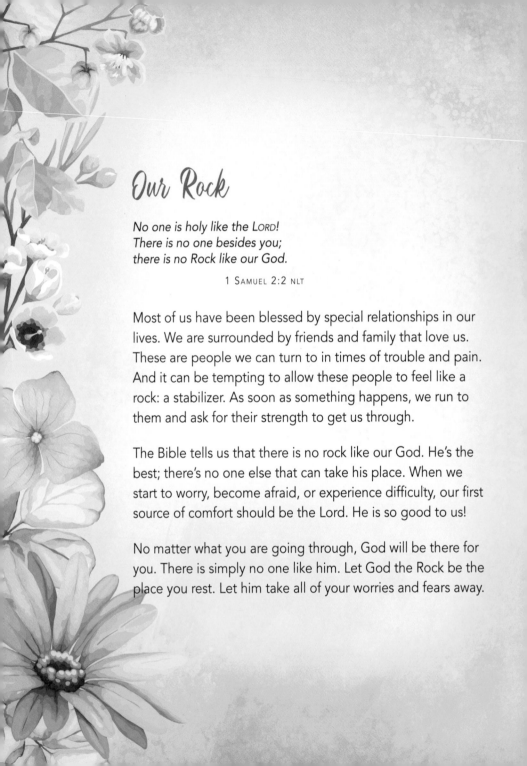

Our Rock

No one is holy like the Lord!
There is no one besides you;
there is no Rock like our God.

1 Samuel 2:2 NLT

Most of us have been blessed by special relationships in our lives. We are surrounded by friends and family that love us. These are people we can turn to in times of trouble and pain. And it can be tempting to allow these people to feel like a rock: a stabilizer. As soon as something happens, we run to them and ask for their strength to get us through.

The Bible tells us that there is no rock like our God. He's the best; there's no one else that can take his place. When we start to worry, become afraid, or experience difficulty, our first source of comfort should be the Lord. He is so good to us!

No matter what you are going through, God will be there for you. There is simply no one like him. Let God the Rock be the place you rest. Let him take all of your worries and fears away.

Can you trust God to be your first source of comfort?

_____
_____
_____
_____
_____
_____
_____
_____
_____
_____
_____
_____
_____
_____
_____
_____
_____
_____
_____
_____
_____
_____

Nothing to Fear

In the day that I'm afraid, I lay all my fears before you
and trust in you with all my heart.
What harm could a man bring to me?
With God on my side I will not be afraid of what comes.
The roaring praises of God fill my heart,
and I will always triumph as I trust his promises.

PSALM 56:3-4 TPT

A loud crash in the night. Unexpected footsteps falling uncomfortably close in a dark parking lot. A ringing phone at 3:00 AM. No matter how brave we think we are, certain situations quicken the pulse. We've heard, over and over, that we have nothing to fear if we walk with God, but let's be honest: certain situations are scary!

At times, it is people that we fear the most. We are afraid of rejection, broken trust, embarrassment, or shame. We want to feel safe, loved, and accepted, but this feels like it comes at a risk. Let's consider David's words from Psalm 56. When we are afraid, and we will be, we can give our situation to God and let him take the fear away. Notice it doesn't say he changes the situation, but that he changes our response to it. We have nothing to fear not because scary things don't exist, but because God erases our worry and replaces it with trust.

You might be anxious about a big event that you are a part of, or maybe you have to engage in a difficult conversation. Maybe you are just nervous because you don't know what a specific day will bring. You can trust God with all your heart. Believe it today.

What are you afraid of?
Have you truly tried letting go of that fear? If not, why?

_____

_____

_____

_____

_____

_____

_____

_____

_____

_____

_____

_____

_____

_____

_____

_____

_____

_____

_____

_____

_____

Mind Games

*Let the peace that Christ gives control your thinking,
because you were called together in one body to have peace.
Always be thankful.*

COLOSSIANS 3:15 NCV

Our minds can be a ballfield with baseball-like thoughts hurtling every which way. Maybe you have your mitt out, ready to catch, or maybe you get hit with a thought out of left field.

Instead of allowing your thoughts to be statements of truth, take thoughts as information, and then determine your response. Learn to quiet your thoughts; don't let them knock you over.

Are your "baseball thoughts" God-honoring? In God's eyes, you are dressed in the righteousness of Christ. Accept that thought as truth and act on it. Dismiss wrong thoughts as a part of your old, sinful nature. Desire peace with other Christians, viewing them as new creations too. Allow your thoughts about them to promote peace among you. Trust God's promise that his peace can control your thoughts.

What's the best way for you to let
the peace of Christ rule your mind?

_____

_____

_____

_____

_____

_____

_____

_____

_____

_____

_____

_____

_____

_____

_____

_____

_____

_____

_____

_____

_____

_____

_____

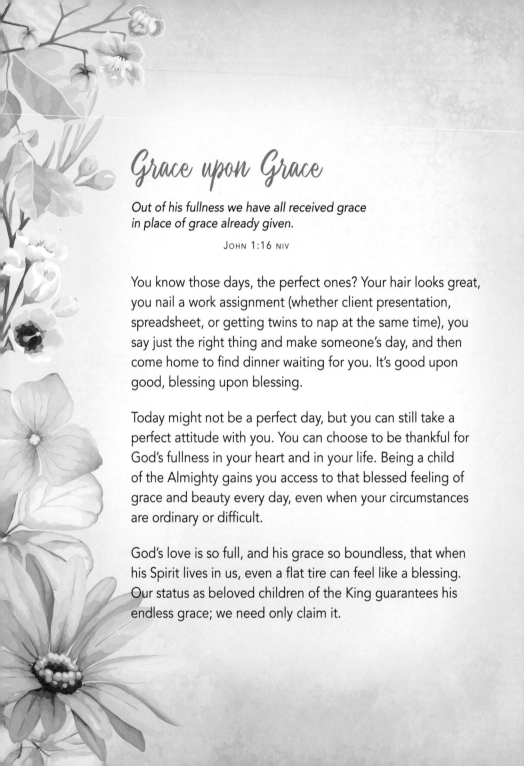

Grace upon Grace

*Out of his fullness we have all received grace
in place of grace already given.*

JOHN 1:16 NIV

You know those days, the perfect ones? Your hair looks great,
you nail a work assignment (whether client presentation,
spreadsheet, or getting twins to nap at the same time), you
say just the right thing and make someone's day, and then
come home to find dinner waiting for you. It's good upon
good, blessing upon blessing.

Today might not be a perfect day, but you can still take a
perfect attitude with you. You can choose to be thankful for
God's fullness in your heart and in your life. Being a child
of the Almighty gains you access to that blessed feeling of
grace and beauty every day, even when your circumstances
are ordinary or difficult.

God's love is so full, and his grace so boundless, that when
his Spirit lives in us, even a flat tire can feel like a blessing.
Our status as beloved children of the King guarantees his
endless grace; we need only claim it.

How have you seen God's grace
poured out on you recently?

_____
_____
_____
_____
_____
_____
_____
_____
_____
_____
_____
_____
_____
_____
_____
_____
_____
_____
_____
_____
_____
_____
_____

In Sunshine and Storm

In the day of prosperity be joyful,
and in the day of adversity consider;
God has made the one as well as the other,
so that mortals may not find out
anything that will come after them.

ECCLESIASTES 7:14 NRSV

It's easy to feel happy on a sunny day, when all is well, the birds are singing, and life is going along swimmingly. But what happens when waters are rougher, bad news comes, or the days feel just plain hard?

God wants us to feel gladness when times are good. He has made each and every day. We are called to rejoice in all of them whether good or bad. Happiness is determined by our circumstances, but true joy comes when we can find the silver linings, hidden in our darkest hours—when we can sing God's praises no matter what.

We don't know what the future holds for us here on earth, but we can find our delight in the knowledge that our eternity is set in the beauty of full relationship with our heavenly Father.

How can you trust God with your future?

_____

_____

_____

_____

_____

_____

_____

_____

_____

_____

_____

_____

_____

_____

_____

_____

_____

_____

_____

_____

_____

_____

_____

Delightful

The Lord takes delight in his people;
he crowns the humble with victory.

PSALM 149:4 NIV

If ever there was something to lift your spirits and get you through the toughest of days, it's the knowledge that God takes delight in you. He tells you so in his Word! He takes pleasure in your very existence. Your heavenly Father created you to be in relationship with him, and he gets great joy out of it. Take that delightful thought with you throughout your day.

Revel in the knowledge of God's delight for you each day. Embrace the fact that there is one who loves you and is truly captivated by you.

God loves spending time with you; he wants to get closer to you. Allow him to take you deeper. Dive in and experience his delight for yourself.

How did you feel God's delight in you today?

_____
_____
_____
_____
_____
_____
_____
_____
_____
_____
_____
_____
_____
_____
_____
_____
_____
_____
_____
_____
_____
_____
_____
_____

Honor in Purity

*The LORD has rewarded me according to my righteousness,
according to the cleanness of my hands in his sight.*

PSALM 18:24 ESV

What do you think of when you hear the word purity?
Perhaps a nun in her convent—someone who keeps herself
completely untouched by the temptations of the world—an
innocent child, or a great religious figure?

Often when we think about purity we think of a lack of
obvious, outward sin. But both purity and impurity are
birthed in the heart and developed in the mind long before
they become expressed in action. Our purity is measured,
not in what we do or what we have done, but in the hidden
places of our heart's attitudes and our mind's wanderings.

If you ever wonder if your purity counts for anything—if
refraining from the pleasures of sin is even worth it—
be encouraged. God will reward you according to your
righteousness. He sees the intentions of your heart and the
thoughts in your mind. He knows how badly you want to
please him with your life, and he will bless you for it. He is
honored in your purity, and that honor is the most important
reward of all.

What attitude or thought pattern might God be trying to shine his light into at this moment?

_____
_____
_____
_____
_____
_____
_____
_____
_____
_____
_____
_____
_____
_____
_____
_____
_____
_____
_____
_____
_____
_____
_____
_____

Swept Into Him

Let that abide in you which you heard from the beginning.
If what you heard from the beginning abides in you,
you also will abide in the Son and in the Father.

1 John 2:24 nasb

Most homes, even those of the most organized among us, end up with junk drawer. Maybe a junk closet, junk room, or a garage you can no longer park in is more your situation. No matter how large your clutter-catcher is, the problem is the same: space. Everything that enters your home needs a spot, and the more that comes in, the fewer the open spaces. Eventually, be it a yard sale, donation, or a storage unit, something's got to go.

Our hearts and minds are basically the same. Everything allowed inside takes up room. One of the most wonderful gifts of a relationship with Jesus is the space his Spirit claims in our lives. The more we invite him in, the more junk gets cleared away. His peace pushes out anxiety. His patience banishes our short temperedness. His joy leaves no room for contention.

The reality of God in us and we in him is beautiful. When he comes to us, we are swept into him. Like a sponge in the ocean, our lives are forever saturated by his goodness.

What does considering your oneness with God do for your heart?

_____
_____
_____
_____
_____
_____
_____
_____
_____
_____
_____
_____
_____
_____
_____
_____
_____
_____
_____
_____
_____
_____
_____

With You

"Fear not, for I am with you;
be not dismayed, for I am your God;
I will strengthen you, I will help you,
I will uphold you with my righteous right hand."

ISAIAH 41:10 ESV

"I am with you." Sometimes, that's all we need to hear, isn't it? It's why we have those special few on speed dial: the friend, the sister, the mentor who says, "I'm here" and instantly the crisis grows smaller. The presence of another—minus even words or touch—is enough to quiet an anxious spirit. And when that "other" is God? What can this, or any day throw at us that we, with his strengthening help, can't handle? Even weak, we are strong. Even trembling, we remain upright. Our God is just that strong, just that for us, just that good. Even on a day that's hard, his arms are waiting.

Think back to your childhood, and a time you were frightened, then calmed. Perhaps Dad shone a flashlight under a bed you were certain housed a monster, revealing instead an old suitcase and a stuffed bear. That mysterious noise turned out to be a tree branch against the eaves, or a squirrel in the rain gutter. Once you understood how safe you were, your fears were even funny.

Take that joyous laughter to any grown-up fears you may be facing. Upheld by God, who never leaves you, you are strong enough to shine the light at anything.

Where do you need God to reveal his presence and quiet a fear?

_____

_____

_____

_____

_____

_____

_____

_____

_____

_____

_____

_____

_____

_____

_____

_____

_____

_____

_____

_____

_____

_____

_____

Very Good Work

The heavens and the earth were finished, and all the host of them. And on the seventh day God finished his work that he had done, and he rested on the seventh day from all his work that he had done.

GENESIS 2:1-2 ESV

It must have taken a lot of energy for God to create this universe, this world, and the complexity that is humanity. God also planned rest into his creative work. After he had finished his very good work he rested.

At the end of a long day it's easy to feel a little down because your energy has been depleted. As you go through your day, your various working activities required energy from you. Think about God's intention for rest after hard work; he knows what is best for you. Take a few moments to rest from your very good work.

You may have had very little time for yourself today, but now you have a moment to sit and reflect on the goodness of God with the idea that he wants you to be here and rest in him.

How can you ensure that you set aside time to rest?

_____
_____
_____
_____
_____
_____
_____
_____
_____
_____
_____
_____
_____
_____
_____
_____
_____
_____
_____
_____
_____
_____

Every Good Thing

Every gift God freely gives us is good and perfect, streaming down from the Father of lights, who shines from the heavens with no hidden shadow or darkness and is never subject to change.

JAMES 1:17 TPT

Is there someone in your life who always seems to come up with the perfect gift? From a scarf that matches your eyes, to a care-package of herbal teas, an empty journal and a beautiful pen, this person just gets you, and so what they give is always just right. Good gift-givers are themselves a gift.

Consider our Lord, and the intimate way he attends to us. What if we could start seeing not just the obvious gifts, but every good thing as a gift from above? Pay special attention today to all the good you see, hear and experience, and consider the Father as the author of it all.

Along with all the good and perfect things about our Father lies this incredible treasure: he never changes! Even the most loving relationships, the most stable job, the most well-behaved child is bound to change. Only one thing is certain, and it's the goodness of our Lord. He simply can't be any other way.

What is the best gift
God gave you today?

_____

_____

_____

_____

_____

_____

_____

_____

_____

_____

_____

_____

_____

_____

_____

_____

_____

_____

_____

_____

_____

_____

_____

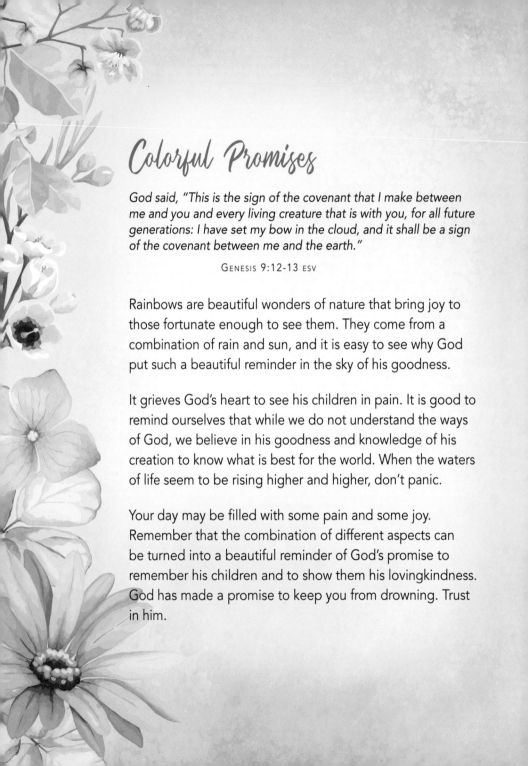

Colorful Promises

God said, "This is the sign of the covenant that I make between me and you and every living creature that is with you, for all future generations: I have set my bow in the cloud, and it shall be a sign of the covenant between me and the earth."

GENESIS 9:12-13 ESV

Rainbows are beautiful wonders of nature that bring joy to those fortunate enough to see them. They come from a combination of rain and sun, and it is easy to see why God put such a beautiful reminder in the sky of his goodness.

It grieves God's heart to see his children in pain. It is good to remind ourselves that while we do not understand the ways of God, we believe in his goodness and knowledge of his creation to know what is best for the world. When the waters of life seem to be rising higher and higher, don't panic.

Your day may be filled with some pain and some joy. Remember that the combination of different aspects can be turned into a beautiful reminder of God's promise to remember his children and to show them his lovingkindness. God has made a promise to keep you from drowning. Trust in him.

What pressure are you feeling today that is causing anxiety? Can you put your trust in God and in his very good promises?

_____
_____
_____
_____
_____
_____
_____
_____
_____
_____
_____
_____
_____
_____
_____
_____
_____
_____
_____
_____
_____
_____
_____

Ripples to Waves

Remember to welcome strangers, because some who have done this have welcomed angels without knowing it.

Hebrews 13:2 NCV

Who is the best hostess you know—that dear soul whose door is always open and whose table is always full? It's not hard to think of someone, is it? The gift of hospitality is easy to recognize and wonderful to benefit from. Perhaps that warm hostess is you: opening your home, filling it with friends, and satisfying their appetites is food for your soul.

While hospitality is a gift of the Spirit, coming to some as naturally as breath, others among us are more inclined to attend than to host. Just the thought of entertaining makes us uncomfortable. The cleaning, the shopping, the cooking, the cleaning again? "I'll bring the bread," we say tentatively. But what might we be missing out on? Who knows who God has sent to help us open our hearts along with our homes?

Won't it be fun to get to heaven and have it all make sense? To see all the interconnected threads, all the ripple effects of every tiny act of kindness? As you end your day, imagine a world where hospitality comes as naturally as breath. See ripples turn to waves as strangers are welcomed as family.

Where in your life can you show greater hospitality?
Does God bring anyone specific to mind?

_____
_____
_____
_____
_____
_____
_____
_____
_____
_____
_____
_____
_____
_____
_____
_____
_____
_____
_____
_____
_____
_____
_____
_____
_____

Blizzard Warning

A wise warning to someone who will listen
is as valuable as gold earrings or fine gold jewelry.

PROVERBS 25:12 NCV

In many climates, it would be unwise to plan a winter road trip without checking the weather report. Even more unwise would be to move forward with your driving plans despite a blizzard warning. Accepting the forecaster's advice to stay put will likely save time, money, and possibly even your life.

Weather reports and wise counselors are just a few of the ways God speaks to us in order to keep us safe and on the path to a good and prosperous life. Whether we listen, though, is entirely up to us. If someone loves us enough to call out a questionable relationship or risky behavior, we would do wise to seriously consider their concerns. The wisdom of a godly friend is truly worth more than gold.

How bold are you when it comes to dispensing godly advice? If the Lord has called something to your attention, prayerfully discern if he wants you to pass it along. Pray for courage to speak up, compassion to speak lovingly, and patience and humility in the event your counsel is rejected. All you can do is speak the truth in love, and then pray for the hearer to listen.

How can you prepare your heart for God to use you to bless someone with your words?

_____
_____
_____
_____
_____
_____
_____
_____
_____
_____
_____
_____
_____
_____
_____
_____
_____
_____
_____
_____
_____

Hard to Resist

Again, the devil took him to a very high mountain and showed him all the kingdoms of the world and their glory. And he said to him, "All these I will give you, if you will fall down and worship me."

MATTHEW 4:8-9 ESV

The world can offer a lot of great things. Careers offer success, relationships offer security, and riches can provide comfort. Nothing is inherently wrong with having these things, unless they are used for our own glory.

In the world, people want to glorify themselves. This is what the devil was after, too. He wanted to be worshiped. Thankfully, Jesus knew that the kingdoms of this world were nothing like the kingdom of God. He chose something greater. Are you able to resist the temptation of the world today?

There are many pressures to serve things other than God's kingdom. Have you found yourself buying something you didn't need? Did you say yes to one more thing because you didn't want to look bad by saying no? We need to reassess our decisions in light of who we are serving. The Bible says we should only worship the Lord our God. Tell the devil who is boss and let God minister to you as you resist temptation.

What is drawing you away from worshiping God alone?

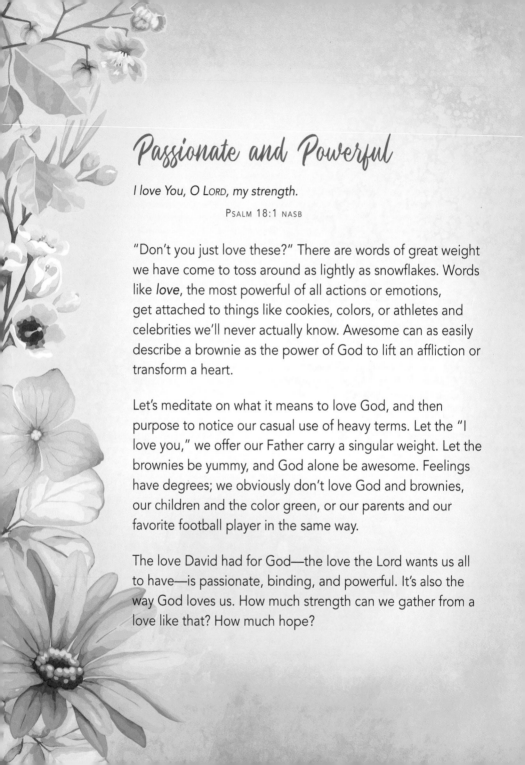

Passionate and Powerful

I love You, O Lᴏʀᴅ, my strength.

Psᴀʟᴍ 18:1 ɴᴀsʙ

"Don't you just love these?" There are words of great weight we have come to toss around as lightly as snowflakes. Words like *love*, the most powerful of all actions or emotions, get attached to things like cookies, colors, or athletes and celebrities we'll never actually know. Awesome can as easily describe a brownie as the power of God to lift an affliction or transform a heart.

Let's meditate on what it means to love God, and then purpose to notice our casual use of heavy terms. Let the "I love you," we offer our Father carry a singular weight. Let the brownies be yummy, and God alone be awesome. Feelings have degrees; we obviously don't love God and brownies, our children and the color green, or our parents and our favorite football player in the same way.

The love David had for God—the love the Lord wants us all to have—is passionate, binding, and powerful. It's also the way God loves us. How much strength can we gather from a love like that? How much hope?

Imagine yourself in a deep, loving embrace
with your Creator. How does it feel?

_____
_____
_____
_____
_____
_____
_____
_____
_____
_____
_____
_____
_____
_____
_____
_____
_____
_____
_____
_____
_____
_____
_____
_____
_____

Empty but Blessed

"Blessed are the poor in spirit, for theirs is the kingdom of heaven. Blessed are those who mourn, for they will be comforted."

MATTHEW 5:3-4 NIV

There are days where you might wake up a little more sluggish, with a little less energy and positivity about the day. That can feel kind of empty, a gap you're hoping to fill. The great thing about the God you serve is that in him, you can be complete. He can be that gap-filler. As you sit with him, his light begins to burn brighter.

On this particular day, meet God in dependence. Come to him even when you don't feel like it. Present your helplessness and emptiness to him and he will bless you and fill your gap with warmth, joy, peace, care, and love.

As you spend time with God, allow him to speak to you and rest knowing you were transformed and filled on one of the hardest days. He is faithful and loving no matter your circumstance or feeling.

Have you seen the fruit of this promise on one of
your rough days? What did that look like?

_____

_____

_____

_____

_____

_____

_____

_____

_____

_____

_____

_____

_____

_____

_____

_____

_____

_____

_____

_____

_____

_____

_____

Selflessness

"Greater love has no one than this:
to lay down one's life for one's friends."

JOHN 15:13 NIV

In a society that seems to grow more self-oriented every day, the New Testament notion of selflessness is certainly counter-cultural. The idea that we would willingly place our own wants below those of our friends, neighbors, and even people half way around the world can be controversial.

What then do we make of this call to selflessness? Are we to skip over it, or, can we look past our first, bristly reaction and find the imbedded gift? The moment we stop thinking about ourselves—start giving ourselves away—is the moment we realize that letting go of "me" is what makes way for "us." Standing up for "my rights" becomes standing up for "our rights." Laying down "my life" means joining with yours and together being swept up into Christ's.

What would you die for? Fortunately for most people, this is a question we'll never need to prove our answer to. It's the stuff of journal writing, or perhaps Bible study conversation, but not a serious decision. And yet, for Jesus, it was. John didn't share these words of Jesus in his Gospel so we'd all rush into burning buildings and otherwise throw ourselves into harm's way to save one another; he shared it so we could try and comprehend the incredible depth of Jesus' love for us.

How selfless do you believe you are? What does laying
your life down for your friends look like for you?

_____
_____
_____
_____
_____
_____
_____
_____
_____
_____
_____
_____
_____
_____
_____
_____
_____
_____
_____
_____
_____
_____
_____
_____
_____
_____

Salt and Light

"You are the salt of the earth. But what good is salt if it has lost its flavor? Can you make it salty again? It will be thrown out and trampled underfoot as worthless. You are the light of the world— like a city on a hilltop that cannot be hidden. No one lights a lamp and then puts it under a basket. Instead, a lamp is placed on a stand, where it gives light to everyone in the house."

MATTHEW 5:13-15 NLT

You are blessed simply because you believe in Jesus and have eternal life. When Jesus was speaking to the disciples, he wanted them to know that this very good thing that they had received needed to be shared.

There is no point to a life in Christ if we lose the one thing that makes us different from the world. God wants you to display a life that shows how wonderful salvation is. As you prepare yourself for bed tonight, the last thing you will probably do is turn out the lights. You need the light to see everything you are doing until then. You need the light to show you the way. There would be no point of turning on the light only to cover it up.

This is our journey of salvation. Jesus didn't want you to receive his light and then hide it. He wants you to shine brightly so others will also see the path to faith. He wants you to be like salt in an otherwise bland world.

Where have you hidden your light lately?
In what situations have you become more bland?

_____

_____

_____

_____

_____

_____

_____

_____

_____

_____

_____

_____

_____

_____

_____

_____

_____

_____

_____

_____

_____

_____

_____

Sleep in Peace

I go to bed and sleep in peace,
because, LORD, only you keep me safe.

PSALM 4:8 NCV

Ah, peace. Just to speak the word starts to bring the feeling on. Long before his birth, Isaiah called Jesus the Prince of Peace, and Jesus himself mentions peace over 100 times in the Bible, so it seems reasonable to believe it's important to him. Most of us would say it's important to us too, but do our lives reflect this? Do we lie down in peace, or do we bring unfinished business, worries, and our phones to bed with us?

As we sleep, does Jesus inhabit our dreams or does the chatter of our busyness continue to occupy us even then? Let us pray for the peace of Christ to rule our thoughts and actions. Regardless of the day, how done the to-do list is, how resolved the issues, we can go to bed and sleep in peace.

We may need to lay our concerns out one by one, giving them over to the Lord and his infinitely-more-capable plans. We may need to shift our minds entirely off ourselves by praying for others or reading the Word. We may simply need to pray, "Lord, bring your peace." The method is not nearly so important as the intention. Let the Prince of Peace rock you to sleep tonight.

How might you tweak your nighttime routine to invite peaceful sleep?

_____

_____

_____

_____

_____

_____

_____

_____

_____

_____

_____

_____

_____

_____

_____

_____

_____

_____

_____

_____

_____

_____

_____

Your Treasure

"Do not lay up for yourselves treasures on earth, where moth and rust destroy and where thieves break in and steal, but lay up for yourselves treasures in heaven, where neither moth nor rust destroys and where thieves do not break in and steal."

MATTHEW 6:19-20 ESV

Have you ever been sitting on a beach and watched a little child work tirelessly on an elaborate sand castle? These little children are unaware of the patterns of ocean waves and don't realize that as the day passes, their masterpieces will eventually be swept away by the swelling tide. All that work, all that concentration, all that pride, gone as the water erases the shore.

What castles are we building in our lives that could, at any moment, be simply erased? We must know what can last and what won't. There are temporary kingdoms and a kingdom that will never pass away. We have to recognize which one we are contributing to.

If your work and your heart are invested in a heavenly vision, then what you have spent your life on will continue to matter for longer than you live. Spend your time investing in the eternal souls of people, in the eternal vision of advancing God's kingdom, and in the never-ending truth of the Gospel. In these things you will find purpose and treasure that will never be lost.

What are you putting your time, energy, and talents into?

_____

_____

_____

_____

_____

_____

_____

_____

_____

_____

_____

_____

_____

_____

_____

_____

_____

_____

_____

_____

_____

_____

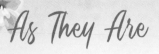

As They Are

Accept one another, then,
just as Christ accepted you,
in order to bring praise to God.

ROMANS 15:7 NIV

It's easy to come up with ways other people could change for the better, isn't it? If she could keep a secret. If he would stop bragging about his possessions. We know Christ calls us to live in harmony with one another, but sometimes others can make this challenging. We start to notice sins and flaws, and the next thing we know, it's all we can see.

Romans 15:7 reminds us to accept one another as Christ accepted us. Broken, imperfect, and sinful, Jesus loves us just as we are. If this is how our Savior feels about us, then truly, who are we to place conditions on our acceptance of one another? Yes, everyone in our lives could improve. But we bring glory to God by loving them as they are.

As much as we might struggle to be more gracious toward a gossipy friend or a neighbor with a bit too much braggadocio, how much more challenging is it to extend that grace to the addict on the corner, or the shockingly rude customer on the phone? How about that politician that gets under your skin? And yet, this is exactly what we are called to do. Jesus loves that dirty, shivering addict as much as he loves us. His heart beats for you and the politician with the same abiding love. How much glory we bring him when we extend grace, acceptance, and love despite agreement or understanding.

Can you think of an opportunity to practice true acceptance?

_____

_____

_____

_____

_____

_____

_____

_____

_____

_____

_____

_____

_____

_____

_____

_____

_____

_____

_____

_____

_____

_____

The Real Prize

"Be strong, and let us be courageous for our people and for the cities of our God; and may the Lord do what seems good to him."

1 Chronicles 19:13 nrsv

Pause for a moment and read the verse aloud. For many of us, the first part of this verse is easy to rally around. Be strong! Have courage! Let's do this! But how about that second half? Can you easily say, "Whatever seems good to you, God" or do you typically struggle for control, ask for certain outcomes, want things to go your way? Is surrender to his plan easy for you, or a constant challenge?

In the words of Joab to his army, we find a perfect model of surrender: be strong for those we serve; be courageous for the Kingdom of God, and may the Lord's will be done. Nothing for us, all for God and those he has given us to serve. Oh, that we could achieve such devotion!

"Your Kingdom come, your will be done, unless it interferes with my happiness." If we were fully honest before God, our version of the Lord's Prayer might sound more like this. What if what he wills for my team to lose? What if he wills the other candidate to get the job? What if God's plan is to grow my character through a season of loss and struggle? This is where courage comes in. As we trust him, we see that it's in the brave fighting we best glorify him.

What cause, issue, or people come to mind when you think of fighting bravely? How can you step in?

_____

_____

_____

_____

_____

_____

_____

_____

_____

_____

_____

_____

_____

_____

_____

_____

_____

_____

_____

_____

_____

_____

_____

Under His Care

"Look at the birds. They don't plant or harvest or store food in barns, for your heavenly Father feeds them. And aren't you far more valuable to him than they are? Can all your worries add a single moment to your life?"

MATTHEW 6:26 NLT

When you wake up in the morning you can begin to feel anxious about the day ahead. What will you wear? What do you need to organize? Will you make it in time to your important appointment?

Life is so full that we can feel overwhelmed with worry about getting it all done and getting it all done right. Jesus didn't want us to feel like that. God cares for us and takes care of a lot of the small things that we probably don't realize he has had a hand in. Recognize his work in your life, and head into it with confidence.

What is it about coming home after a long day that makes us want to change into something more comfortable? Sometimes we need to be reminded that we even have this option. We are privileged that God not only looks after our basic needs but often blesses us with more.

What blessings are you thankful for?
Where can you see God's provision in your life?

_____

_____

_____

_____

_____

_____

_____

_____

_____

_____

_____

_____

_____

_____

_____

_____

_____

_____

_____

_____

_____

_____

_____

_____

Hope in the Storm

"All who listen to my instructions and follow them are wise, like a man who builds his house on solid rock. Though the rain comes in torrents, and the floods rise and the storm winds beat against his house, it won't collapse, for it is built on rock."

MATTHEW 7:24-25 TLB

Jesus didn't just give instructions on how to live so we could be nice people. There are nice people everywhere: believers and unbelievers alike. He gave us ways to live so we could walk through the storms with peace and joy in our hearts. Our confidence is not in everything that is happening around us; it is in knowing that with Christ we have a new, eternal life. That knowledge is our solid foundation.

When we ignore God's ways, we also ignore the hope that he has placed in our hearts for his eternal kingdom. Forgetting to live with this eternal perspective means that even the smallest of storms can beat us down, making us feel discouraged and hopeless.

As you take this time to think, reflect on whether you have been facing your challenges with hope or despair.

How have you been responding to the storms of life?

Ready to See

Open my eyes that I may see wonderful things in your law.
Psalm 119:18 NIV

Have you ever been the last person to get a joke? As everyone else wiped tears of laughter from their eyes, you smiled and thought, "Huh?" But then, suddenly, the extra layer of meaning was illuminated and your laughter became as genuine as everyone else's. Or maybe, seeing an old movie through adult eyes, you understand why your parents didn't want you watching it as a child.

We call these "aha" moments, and Bible reading provides an endless series of them. As we go deeper into the Word, God opens our eyes to fresh revelations, allowing stories we thought we knew to become fresh and exciting. Passages we've taken for granted take on sudden weight and significance when the Lord opens our eyes.

As a little girl, it may not have made sense to you that you couldn't have cake for breakfast, lunch, and dinner. By the time you reached a certain age, though, you understood the wisdom of this rule. Speed limits can feel like a nuisance, especially to a young driver, but as we gain experience, we appreciate the safety of slower-moving cars in neighborhoods and around blind curves. So it is with God's law. The more he illuminates our understanding, the more we understand that every command is handed down in love. Every rule is designed with our best life in mind.

Is there a Scripture you struggle to embrace?
Can you see God's loving intention in it?

_____

_____

_____

_____

_____

_____

_____

_____

_____

_____

_____

_____

_____

_____

_____

_____

_____

_____

_____

_____

_____

_____

Find Peace Here

*Those of steadfast mind you keep in peace
because they trust in you.*

ISAIAH 26:3 NRSV

If you were to form a mental picture of chaos, what would you see? Impossible deadlines, commitments on top of commitments, long lists and short hours? How about peace? What picture comes to mind? Most of us picture getting away. Whether our minds took us to a hot bath or a tropical island, we're definitely not here. The trouble with this image, though it's wonderful, is that it's fleeting. Whether bathtub or Bali, we can't stay.

Rather than going to a peaceful place, let's start over, inviting peace right into our chaos. Let the Holy Spirit quiet your movements. Let Jesus shift your thoughts. Imagining a place where cares were few and all was quiet, chaos diminished. God promises this peace can be ours any time, any place, anywhere. How? By thinking of him.

Fixing our thoughts on the Lord and all his goodness, we see it is simply impossible to remain unsettled. The more we train our minds to stay with him, the more perfect peace is ours—no matter the circumstances. The more we place our trust in him, the less we have to steal our peace.

What is stealing your peace
and keeping you from trusting Jesus?

_____

_____

_____

_____

_____

_____

_____

_____

_____

_____

_____

_____

_____

_____

_____

_____

_____

_____

_____

_____

_____

Defeating the Mighty

We have this treasure in jars of clay to show that this all-surpassing power is from God and not from us.

2 CORINTHIANS 4:7 NIV

In the age of social media, every day brings another inspiring story. Here's a theme we're probably all familiar with: someone displays miraculous strength, saving someone else. A mother saves her toddler by lifting a car. A man saves a buddy by moving a 500-pound boulder. A vacationing couple swims out into a riptide, saving a drowning stranger. It's such a lovely image, the tiny defeating the mighty.

When our frail, fragile bodies do things they shouldn't be able to, it's because God is able. And it doesn't have to be lifting a car. For some of us, not lifting that glass to our lips or partaking in workplace gossip is a feat of equally miraculous strength. Either way, it's a chance to bring God glory.

When God calls us out of our comfort zone, our first instinct is often to think of all the reasons we can't. Or shouldn't. Or just plain won't. We dwell on our capacity, forgetting the One who calls us is the same one who will equip us. We are like Esther, wondering, "What if I fail?" We are like Moses, saying, "I'm not even a good speaker!" But that's the point, isn't it? The weaker we are, the stronger God is. The more unlikely the hero, the more the signs point upward.

Do you have a crazy, impossible dream that just won't go away? Could God be inviting you to display his glory?

_____

_____

_____

_____

_____

_____

_____

_____

_____

_____

_____

_____

_____

_____

_____

_____

_____

_____

_____

_____

_____

_____

_____

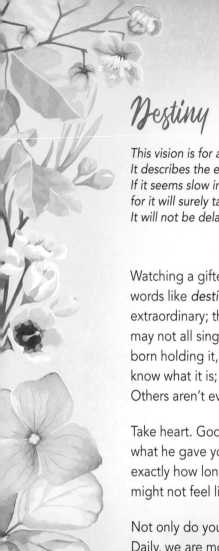

Destiny

This vision is for a future time.
It describes the end, and it will be fulfilled.
If it seems slow in coming, wait patiently,
for it will surely take place.
It will not be delayed.

HABAKKUK 2:3 NLT

Watching a gifted athlete, or listening to a brilliant singer, words like *destiny* come to mind. Some talents are so extraordinary; they simply have to be used and shared. We may not all sing like angels or swing a golf club like we were born holding it, but we do all have a destiny. Some of us know what it is; we're just not ready. The timing isn't right. Others aren't even sure we have one.

Take heart. God knows exactly why he made you. He knows what he gave you to do, and who he gave you to love, and exactly how long it's going to be before you fulfill his plans. It might not feel like it today, but you're right on schedule.

Not only do you have a destiny, but all of humanity does. Daily, we are moving toward a promised end, where heaven and earth are renewed and we will live together with God forever. Whether you long for this day, or whether eternity seldom crosses your mind, allow this promise to assure you: what God promises, God delivers. If something feels late, or even forgotten, know that it is not. His timing is perfect and his love is boundless.

Does God's timing feel slow in an area of your life?
What reason might he have for waiting?

_____
_____
_____
_____
_____
_____
_____
_____
_____
_____
_____
_____
_____
_____
_____
_____
_____
_____
_____
_____
_____
_____
_____
_____
_____
_____

Called to Follow

As Jesus passed along the Sea of Galilee, he saw Simon and his brother Andrew casting a net into the sea—for they were fishermen. And Jesus said to them, "Follow me and I will make you fish for people."

MARK 1:16-17 NKJV

Simon and Andrew were just doing their ordinary job when Jesus called out to them. It wasn't like they were doing anything particularly special. Jesus must have known that they longed for significance in their lives. He put his call to them in their language. They knew that catching fish was sometimes difficult and that it required determination and strength.

This is what the Christian life is like for us. It is sometimes difficult. Think of Jesus calling out to you as your do your ordinary things today. He wants you to follow him into a life full of significance. The disciples responded immediately to Jesus' call to follow him. They must have known about Jesus and his ministry, and they were eager to be a part of God's work on earth.

In our busy lives we can be quick to dismiss Jesus' voice, or it can be drowned out in the noise of everything else competing for our time and energy. As you take some time to stop and still your heart, listen for what Jesus wants to say to you and commit to responding quickly.

What can you hear Jesus speaking to you in this moment?

_____
_____
_____
_____
_____
_____
_____
_____
_____
_____
_____
_____
_____
_____
_____
_____
_____
_____
_____
_____
_____
_____
_____
_____
_____

Moment of Solitude

In the morning, having risen a long while before daylight, He went out and departed to a solitary place; and there He prayed.

MARK 1:35 NKJV

When do you find time to pray? Even if we are intentional and passionate about prayer, the everyday activities in our life will almost always take priority over time with God. It is often said that prayer can happen at any time, and of course it does, but is there value in setting aside a specific time to communicate with God?

Did you ever realize that the notion of quiet times comes from the example set by Jesus? We see in the Bible that Jesus would get up before daylight and pray in a solitary place. We are not often told what Jesus prayed about. It's not the content that matters; it's the willingness to maintain our relationship with the Father and seek his will.

Does this sound like you as you try to step away from the busyness of the day? Are people looking for you, pressing in on your alone time? Instead of trying to fit prayer into your busy day, pray before it gets busy, so you can cope with the pressures of life. Fight for your time with God. Be like Jesus and find time to wait on the Father.

How will you fit prayer time into your busy life?

_____

_____

_____

_____

_____

_____

_____

_____

_____

_____

_____

_____

_____

_____

_____

_____

_____

_____

_____

_____

_____

_____

One Step at a Time

To him who is able to keep you from stumbling and to present you blameless before the presence of his glory with great joy, to the only God, our Savior, through Jesus Christ our Lord, be glory, majesty, dominion, and authority.

JUDE 24-25 ESV

This race called life is a tiring one; sometimes the road gets long and our legs threaten to buckle underneath heavy burdens. How, then, do we persevere? Hear this glorious news: God, whose majesty is matchless, is waiting to hold you up under the weight you are carrying. He lifts the burden to his own strong shoulders. He keeps you from slipping and falling away. He brings you into his presence!

When the cold rains of sorrow or the sharp winds of discouragement are at our backs, how do we press on and finish the race?

Run your race listening to the encouragement of your heavenly Father—his mighty shouts of everlasting joy! Take it one holy step at a time. Keep your eyes on him, and you will finish victorious.

Listen for God's encouraging voice as you take one step at a time. What do you hear him saying to you?

_____
_____
_____
_____
_____
_____
_____
_____
_____
_____
_____
_____
_____
_____
_____
_____
_____
_____
_____
_____
_____
_____
_____
_____
_____

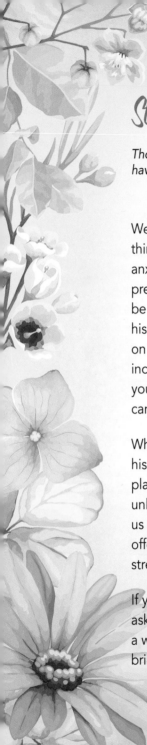

Stress

*Those who love your instructions
have great peace and do not stumble.*

PSALM 119:165 NLT

We are all well acquainted with stress. There are so many things in our lives that cause us to be worried, pressured, and anxious. The world constantly presents us with unknowns and predicaments that steal our joy and rob our peace. You might be facing some of those predicaments today. Spend time in his presence, letting his peace wash over your heart. Focus on his truth and his capability rather than your problems and incapacity. God is able to take everything that is troubling you today and exchange it for peace that is beyond what you can imagine.

When we get in the presence of God and spend time in his Word, we are able to escape the stress of our lives and place our problems in his hands. God gives a peace that is unlike anything the world offers. He is focused on preparing us for his permanent kingdom, and, as a result, his presence offers hope and everlasting joy that is opposite to the trivial stressors of this life.

If you are feeling weary and a little down-trodden tonight, ask God for his guidance. He loves you enough to show you a way through your troubles and stress. Let his love for you bring peace deep within your being.

In what ways is the Lord directing you through your worries and stress?

_____

_____

_____

_____

_____

_____

_____

_____

_____

_____

_____

_____

_____

_____

_____

_____

_____

_____

_____

_____

_____

_____

Loss of Control

My flesh and my heart fail;
But God is the strength of my heart
and my portion forever.

Psalm 73:26 NKJV

Have you ever had a moment where you've felt completely out of control? A car accident, a diagnosis, or some other frightening moment? There are instances in our lives when our own flesh fails us. We recognize in a flash that we are no longer in control of our own outcome—and it terrifies us. In that moment, when control is lost and fear overcomes us, there is one thing we can know for certain. God is our strength, and he never loses control.

There are times when we feel strong and independent and there are times when we realize that we are completely dependent on others. God gave us gifts and strengths but we are still finite creatures. At times, we just have to admit that we can't do it all on our own.

The Psalmist recognized this and acknowledged that God is the source of strength. When your life, and the outcome of it, is ripped from your hands, it's still resting firmly in his grasp. He is your portion. He is your ration. He is enough. Release yourself into the control of the only one who will never lose control.

What have you been trying to do all on your own? How can you rely more on God?

_____

_____

_____

_____

_____

_____

_____

_____

_____

_____

_____

_____

_____

_____

_____

_____

_____

_____

_____

_____

_____

_____

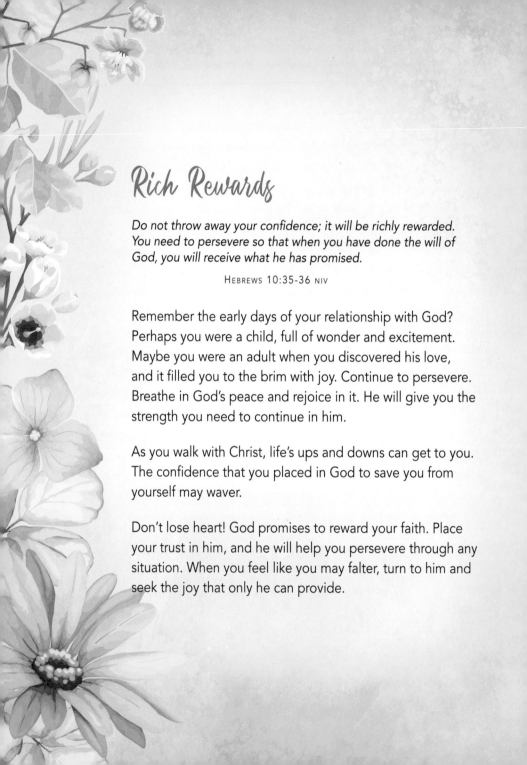

Rich Rewards

Do not throw away your confidence; it will be richly rewarded.
You need to persevere so that when you have done the will of
God, you will receive what he has promised.

HEBREWS 10:35-36 NIV

Remember the early days of your relationship with God?
Perhaps you were a child, full of wonder and excitement.
Maybe you were an adult when you discovered his love,
and it filled you to the brim with joy. Continue to persevere.
Breathe in God's peace and rejoice in it. He will give you the
strength you need to continue in him.

As you walk with Christ, life's ups and downs can get to you.
The confidence that you placed in God to save you from
yourself may waver.

Don't lose heart! God promises to reward your faith. Place
your trust in him, and he will help you persevere through any
situation. When you feel like you may falter, turn to him and
seek the joy that only he can provide.

Where is your confidence today?

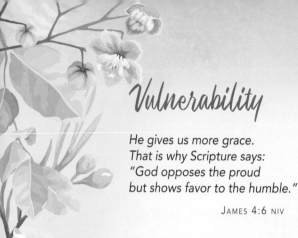

Vulnerability

He gives us more grace.
That is why Scripture says:
"God opposes the proud
but shows favor to the humble."

JAMES 4:6 NIV

Some of the most substantial and ultimately wonderful changes in our lives come from moments of vulnerability: laying our cards on the table, so to speak, and letting someone else know how much they really mean to us. But vulnerability takes one key ingredient: humility. And humility is not easy.

Isn't it sometimes easier for us to pretend that conflict never happened than to face the fact that we made a mistake and wronged another person? It's not always easy to humble ourselves and fight for the resolution in an argument—especially when it means admitting our failures. The wrong kind of pride is not pretty. We are more likely to listen to those who are honest about their situation than those who are trying to make excuses for it. Do you know people who are too proud to admit their mistakes and who blame their failures on others?

Who are you in the face of conflict? Do you avoid apologizing in an attempt to save face? Does your pride get in the way of vulnerability, or are you willing and ready to humble yourself for restoration in your relationships? God says that he will give favor and wisdom to the humble.

What can you do this week to humble yourself
for the sake of a restored relationship?

_____

_____

_____

_____

_____

_____

_____

_____

_____

_____

_____

_____

_____

_____

_____

_____

_____

_____

_____

_____

_____

Eternal Kingdom

Let us be thankful, because we have a kingdom that cannot be shaken. We should worship God in a way that pleases him with respect and fear.

HEBREWS 12:28 NCV

Kings and queens hold their throne for a time, but ultimately their reign ends, either through defeat or death. The kingdom of God is not like the kingdom of men. It is undefeatable and unshakeable.

You belong to God's kingdom, and it will never be defeated. His power will not be surpassed by any other principality or power. Be thankful that you belong to this kingdom. Take heart that the king you worship will be on the throne forever! Worship him as he deserves.

God is the king of this universe and the king of your heart. As you reflect on his majesty, worship him in awe for all he has created and all he has done.

What does an unshakeable kingdom look like in your mind?

_____
_____
_____
_____
_____
_____
_____
_____
_____
_____
_____
_____
_____
_____
_____
_____
_____
_____
_____
_____
_____
_____
_____

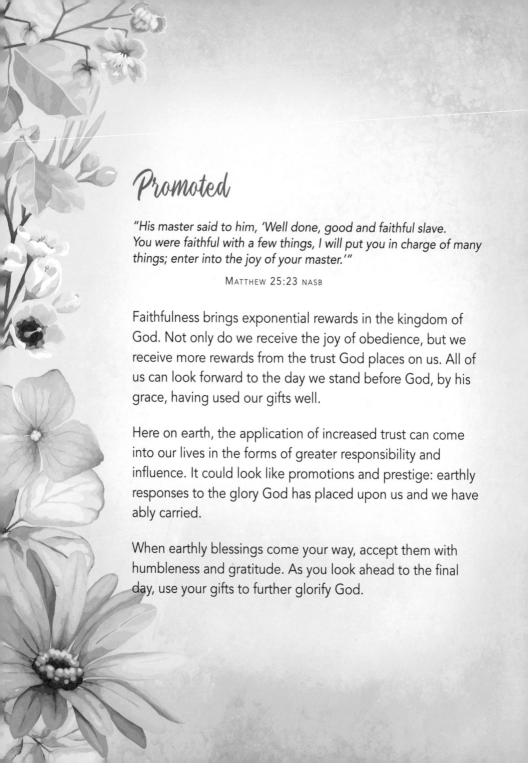

Promoted

*"His master said to him, 'Well done, good and faithful slave.
You were faithful with a few things, I will put you in charge of many
things; enter into the joy of your master.'"*

MATTHEW 25:23 NASB

Faithfulness brings exponential rewards in the kingdom of
God. Not only do we receive the joy of obedience, but we
receive more rewards from the trust God places on us. All of
us can look forward to the day we stand before God, by his
grace, having used our gifts well.

Here on earth, the application of increased trust can come
into our lives in the forms of greater responsibility and
influence. It could look like promotions and prestige: earthly
responses to the glory God has placed upon us and we have
ably carried.

When earthly blessings come your way, accept them with
humbleness and gratitude. As you look ahead to the final
day, use your gifts to further glorify God.

What gifts do you use frequently?

Grief

Your promise revives me;
it comforts me in all my troubles.

PSALM 119:50 NLT

Grief is a strange thing. It shows up in the oddest of places.
As time passes, it becomes threaded into your life in a subtle
way you don't quite notice at first. When you smile and
feel real joy but at the same moment tears spring to your
eyes, that's when you know that grief is not absent even in
happiness.

As time passes and life goes on, we must learn to bear all our
varying emotions in sync. We can smile, we can laugh, and
we can be perfectly happy, but the ache of grief is still there
deep down. We don't forget it, but we don't betray that
which we grieve by smiling either.

As a child of God, you have been promised a hope that
has the power to revive you even in the most sorrowful
of moments. And though your pain is real, deep, and
sometimes overwhelming, your God is strong and able to
lift you out of the deepest pit, and—even when it's hard to
imagine—give you joy. Ask God for joy in the middle of your
grief. Ask for moments of laughter and peace in places you
would least expect to find them.

What grief or trouble are you experiencing right now? Can you let God in?

_____
_____
_____
_____
_____
_____
_____
_____
_____
_____
_____
_____
_____
_____
_____
_____
_____
_____
_____
_____
_____
_____

Thirsty for Mercy

"Come, all you who are thirsty, come to the waters;
and you who have no money, come, buy and eat!
Come, buy wine and milk without money and without cost."

ISAIAH 55:1 NIV

Money is used for what we want, but mostly for the things that we need—like food and even water. Imagine walking into a grocery store and being offered anything you want without having to pay a cent! This is a picture of the mercy that Jesus has shown all of us through his sacrifice.

We need God's mercy in the same way that we thirst for water. Wine and milk were expensive items in the time this was written, and to offer these free of charge would have been a great sacrifice.

What Christ did for you on the cross came at a great price, but it was all because of his great love for you. Embrace the free gift of forgiveness and rest in freedom. Think about God's amazing gifts as you go through each day. If that doesn't put a smile on your face, what else could?

How have you seen God's mercy in your life lately?

_____

_____

_____

_____

_____

_____

_____

_____

_____

_____

_____

_____

_____

_____

_____

_____

_____

_____

_____

_____

_____

_____

Giving Thanks

Enter his gates with thanksgiving
and his courts with praise;
give thanks to him and praise his name.

PSALM 100:4 NIV

The morning alarms came too soon today. Whether they
were in the form of children, an alarm clock, or a heavy heart
that is restless, your slumber is over. Your mind immediately
starts going over your to-do list for the day as you stumble
through your morning routine. You glance at your watch.
How can you already be running late?

It is at this moment that you must stop to thank God.
That's right, actually stop what you are doing, get down on
your knees (to ensure you are stopping), and thank him.
Pausing to thank God gives him the honor he's due, but it
also kisses your heart with peace and joy in the midst of busy
morning routines.

A thankful heart prepares the way for you to connect rightly
with God's heart. He isn't someone we use to get what we
want. He is a sincere, loving provider for everything we will
ever need. Spend some time singing praise to God. Thank
him for this day, no matter how hectic, sad, or boring it might
be. And if it looks to be a great day, tell him that too! He
loves to hear your praise.

Write a poem of thanksgiving to God today.

_____
_____
_____
_____
_____
_____
_____
_____
_____
_____
_____
_____
_____
_____
_____
_____
_____
_____
_____
_____
_____

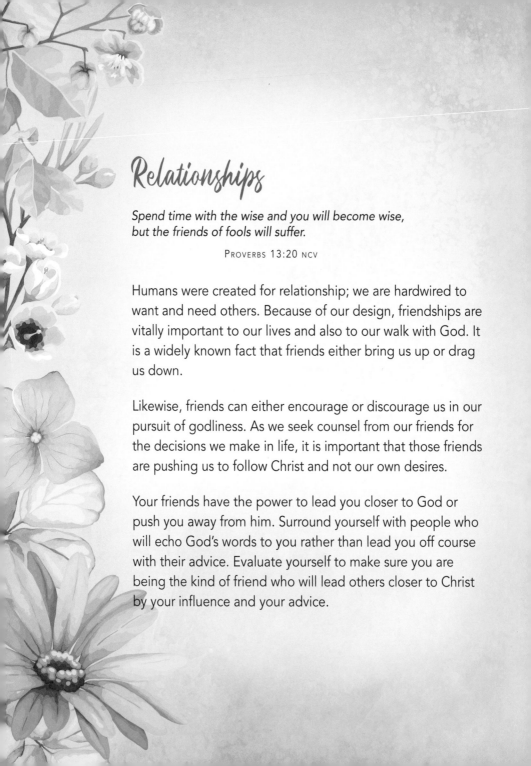

Relationships

Spend time with the wise and you will become wise,
but the friends of fools will suffer.

PROVERBS 13:20 NCV

Humans were created for relationship; we are hardwired to want and need others. Because of our design, friendships are vitally important to our lives and also to our walk with God. It is a widely known fact that friends either bring us up or drag us down.

Likewise, friends can either encourage or discourage us in our pursuit of godliness. As we seek counsel from our friends for the decisions we make in life, it is important that those friends are pushing us to follow Christ and not our own desires.

Your friends have the power to lead you closer to God or push you away from him. Surround yourself with people who will echo God's words to you rather than lead you off course with their advice. Evaluate yourself to make sure you are being the kind of friend who will lead others closer to Christ by your influence and your advice.

Who can you spend time with that encourages you in your relationship with God?

_____
_____
_____
_____
_____
_____
_____
_____
_____
_____
_____
_____
_____
_____
_____
_____
_____
_____
_____
_____
_____
_____
_____
_____
_____

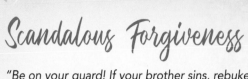

Scandalous Forgiveness

"Be on your guard! If your brother sins, rebuke him; and if he repents, forgive him. And if he sins against you seven times a day, and returns to you seven times, saying, 'I repent,' forgive him."

LUKE 17:3-4 NASB

There are few things worse than being unjustly wronged. It's not easy when you are hurt—especially by someone close to you. A deep part of each of us cries out for justice. It's a God-given trait, meant to call us to stand in the gap for the hurting, the widow, the orphan—it's our longing for true religion. When we identify injustice, that longing rises up strongly. We feel pain, hurt, confusion, and pressure. And more than all those emotions, we feel the deep need to see justice served.

Forgive—over and over again. This is the scandal of the Gospel. This is the very essence of the Jesus we follow. Someone wrongs you? Forgive him. He wrongs you again? Forgive again. But he was wrong. He was sinful. She hurt me deeply. The answer is the same: forgive. Forgiveness is handing the hurt to God and leaving the judgement to him.

We have been forgiven much; therefore, we must love much. No matter how hard it is to forgive someone who has hurt you, remember how much you have been forgiven. How can you extend any less grace than that which you have received?

Who do you need to forgive today?

_____

_____

_____

_____

_____

_____

_____

_____

_____

_____

_____

_____

_____

_____

_____

_____

_____

_____

_____

_____

_____

_____

_____

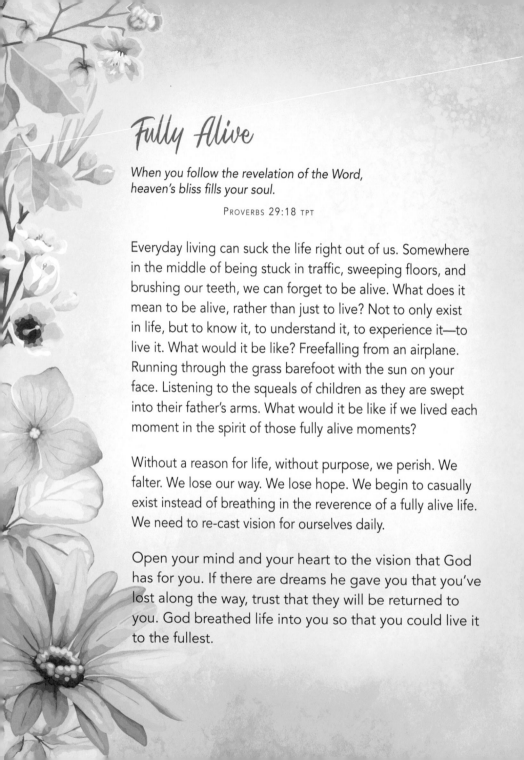

Fully Alive

*When you follow the revelation of the Word,
heaven's bliss fills your soul.*

Proverbs 29:18 TPT

Everyday living can suck the life right out of us. Somewhere in the middle of being stuck in traffic, sweeping floors, and brushing our teeth, we can forget to be alive. What does it mean to be alive, rather than just to live? Not to only exist in life, but to know it, to understand it, to experience it—to live it. What would it be like? Freefalling from an airplane. Running through the grass barefoot with the sun on your face. Listening to the squeals of children as they are swept into their father's arms. What would it be like if we lived each moment in the spirit of those fully alive moments?

Without a reason for life, without purpose, we perish. We falter. We lose our way. We lose hope. We begin to casually exist instead of breathing in the reverence of a fully alive life. We need to re-cast vision for ourselves daily.

Open your mind and your heart to the vision that God has for you. If there are dreams he gave you that you've lost along the way, trust that they will be returned to you. God breathed life into you so that you could live it to the fullest.

What do you need God to breathe life back into?

_____

_____

_____

_____

_____

_____

_____

_____

_____

_____

_____

_____

_____

_____

_____

_____

_____

_____

_____

_____

_____

_____

_____

Never Too Late

Behold, the LORD's hand is not so short
That it cannot save;
Nor is His ear so dull
That it cannot hear.

ISAIAH 59:1 NASB

Do you have regrets in your life that you wish you could take back? Things that you aren't proud of? You lay awake at night thinking about mistakes you've made and you wonder if you've gone too far to ever get back.

When Jesus hung on the cross, there were two thieves hanging beside him. One of those thieves, as he hung in his final moments of life, asked Jesus for grace and a second chance. That thief—minutes before death—was given forgiveness and eternal life. The very same day he entered paradise as a forgiven and clean man. In light of his story, how can we ever say that it's too late to turn it all around?

If you feel like it's too late to change something in your life for the better, remember the story of the thief on the cross. There is always hope in Jesus. The God you serve is the God of second chances. That might sound cliché, but it couldn't be more true. His love has no end and his grace knows no boundary. It is never too late for you to follow him with your life.

What do you need
to be saved from today?

_____

_____

_____

_____

_____

_____

_____

_____

_____

_____

_____

_____

_____

_____

_____

_____

_____

_____

_____

_____

_____

_____

_____

_____

_____

_____

Rebuilt

"I love you people with a love that will last forever.
That is why I have continued showing you kindness.
People of Israel, I will build you up again,
and you will be rebuilt.
You will pick up your tambourines again
and dance with those who are joyful."

JEREMIAH 31:3-4 NCV

We were originally created to bear the mark of our Creator. We were masterfully designed to reflect his image and to reveal his glory. The corruption of sin has masked us, disguising our initial intended purpose. When we respond to salvation and give ourselves back to God, he begins reworking us to once again appear as he intended.

Sanctification is a process that can be painful. But its end result is beautiful. God empties our hearts of the things that could never satisfy us to make room for himself—the only thing that will always satisfy.

There are times in life, perhaps even today, where you feel like God has taken a wrecking ball to your life. He has flattened everything you had—your desires, your interests, your pursuits—but fear not. He will rebuild you. He is creating a masterpiece with your life that will bring him glory and honor. Everything God removes he will restore to mirror the image of his likeness—your intended created purpose.

What do you feel has been broken in your life?
Can you trust God to rebuild you?

_____
_____
_____
_____
_____
_____
_____
_____
_____
_____
_____
_____
_____
_____
_____
_____
_____
_____
_____
_____
_____
_____
_____
_____

New Life

We died and were buried with Christ by baptism. And just as Christ was raised from the dead by the glorious power of the Father, now we also may live new lives.

ROMANS 6:4 NLT

The entire human race is living on borrowed time. We spend our lives with the innate knowledge that we never know when it will all end for us. Death comes, as it always does, to every man.

When it came to Jesus, death didn't have the final say. And in that death—the one death that represented all humanity—the greatest form of life was born. The Gospel truth is that Jesus' death wasn't just a man's life ending on a cross. It was the death to end all deaths. Jesus died and took the full wrath of a righteous God upon himself so that our death sentences would no longer be ours to serve. And the story doesn't end there. The most glorious part of all is his resurrection: his conquering of death, and the ultimate display of power, glory, victory, and grace.

The whole point of the entire Gospel, summed up in one life giving phrase is this: you can have new life. Life that doesn't run out, expire, or end. This beautiful truth isn't just a charming thought. It's your reality as a Christian. By accepting the finished story of the Gospel, you are written into the best ending in existence. Life is yours—glorious, powerful life. Ponder that for a while.

What impacts you the most about the saving work of Christ?

_____

_____

_____

_____

_____

_____

_____

_____

_____

_____

_____

_____

_____

_____

_____

_____

_____

_____

_____

Heaven's Promise

"He will wipe away all tears from their eyes,
and there shall be no more death,
nor sorrow, nor crying, nor pain.
All that has gone forever."

REVELATION 21:4 NLT

When terrible things happen in this world, people cry out to God in desperation. They ask how he could have let it happen. How could the one who is in control of everything possibly be good when there is so much hardship? But when we look at the system of heaven, we realize that God never intended for us to have sorrow, pain, or death. All these things only exist as a result of man's sin.

When the kingdom of heaven is established on earth, we will live as God intended. All wrong will be righted and all pain will disappear. It is good to live and love with eternity's values in mind. On some days, it can be the difference between despair or hope.

As a child of God, you know that any pain you have in this life is temporary because your eternal home will be devoid of it all. When the pain and sadness of the world threatens to overwhelm you, cling to the promise of heaven and the hope that one day every tear will be wiped from your eyes.

What do you feel when you think about all wrongs being righted and all pain being gone?

_____

_____

_____

_____

_____

_____

_____

_____

_____

_____

_____

_____

_____

_____

_____

_____

_____

_____

_____

_____

_____

_____

We're Already In

When you live a life of abandoned love,
surrendered before the awe of God,
here's what you'll experience: Abundant life.
Continual protection.
And complete satisfaction!

PROVERBS 19:23 TPT

As advertisements go, Proverbs 19:23 puts forth a rather persuasive pitch for joining your life to God's. Abundant life? Yes, please! Continual protection? Let us in! Complete satisfaction? Where do we sign? Here's the best part of all: we already signed. We're already in. The day we fell in love with Jesus and asked him into our hearts, all this and more was ours. To claim it, we need only remain in his love. To experience it, we need only give the Father our awe.

When we are reclined on the beach, hearing gentle waves rhythmically hit the shore, the ocean doesn't seem particularly fearsome. Jumping from a ship into twelve-foot swells and with no land in sight? It's hard to imagine anything more terrifying. It's a matter of perspective. From land, it's easy to forget the ocean's vastness and power. From the center, it's impossible to think of anything else.

This is what it means to fear God. To fear him is to respect him—to remember his vastness, to stand in awe of his power. Let us remain at the center of our faith, constantly aware of all he can, has, and will do, and find our secure rest there.